THE HERITAGE COLLECTION

# QUEEN AMINA

Rosemond Sarpong Owens

Illustrated By Amina Yaqoob

Queen Amina

Copyright © 2021 by Rosemond Sarpong Owens

Illustrator: Amina Yaqoob

Library of Congress Control Number: 2021913810



Published by Lion's Historian Press
https://www.lionshistorian.net/

# CONTENTS

# DEDICATION

To my childhood friends,

Yemisi, Bola and Bisi

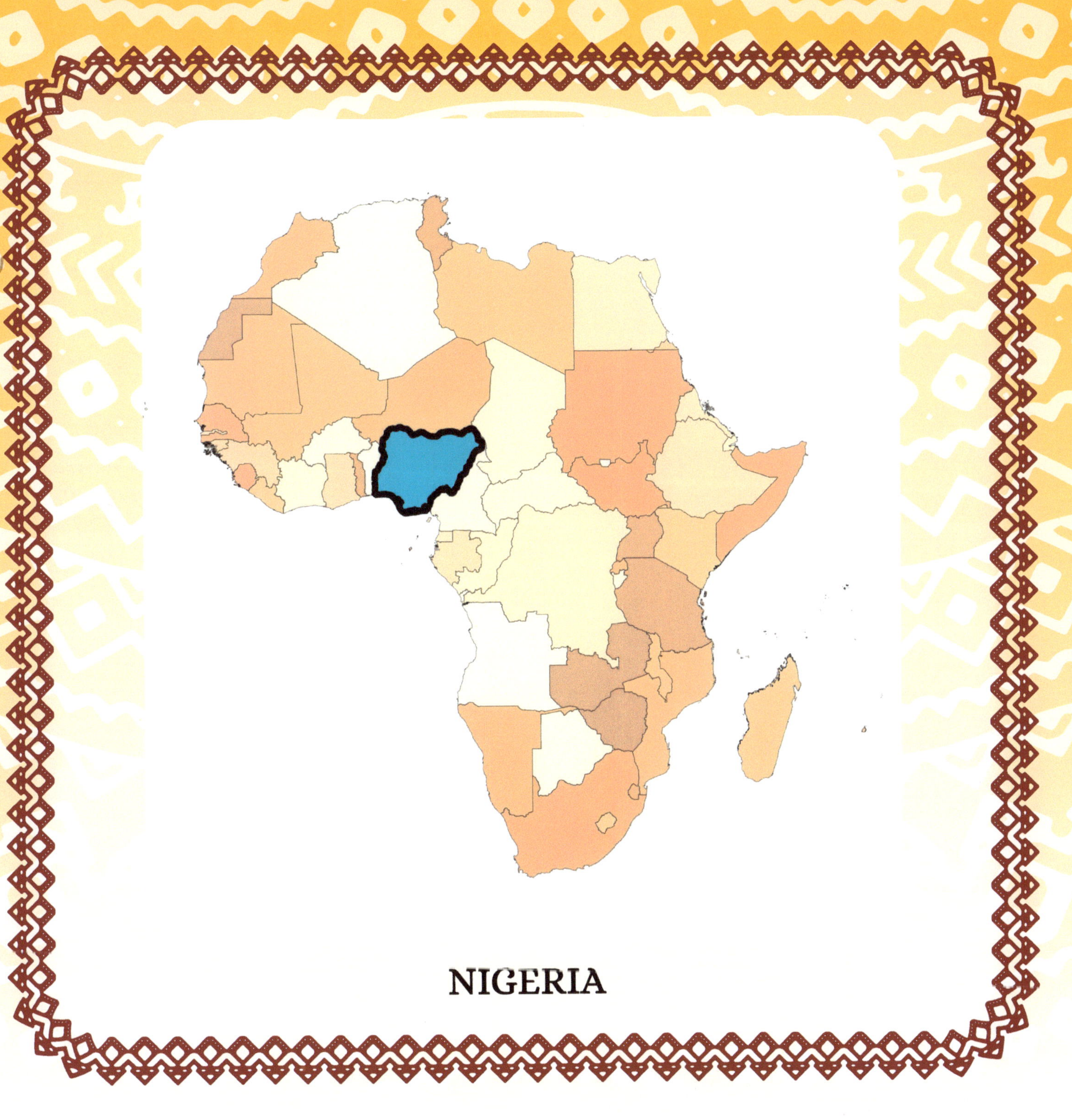

NIGERIA

It was a very cold morning in Zazzau in the year 1533. There was a frenzied atmosphere in the palace; maids were bustling up and down. From one of the huts, shrill cries pierced the air. Queen Bakwa Turunku was about to give birth to a trailblazer.

The queen gave birth to a lovely baby girl, and she was named 'Aminatu', meaning 'peace, loyal, faithful, honest, trustworthy'.

Amina, as she was fondly called, was the eldest child of her parents. Her birth had been highly celebrated by the royal family of Zazzau. Zazzau, now called 'Zaria', was a city-state in the Kingdom of Hausa. It was located somewhere between the Niger River and Lake Chad in modern-day Nigeria. It was ruled by King Nikatau and Queen Bakwa Turunku.

Amina grew up with her two siblings, a younger brother named Karama, and a sister named Zaria.

Amina was brilliant.

Although the young girls of that era did mostly housework, she was treated differently.  As she grew older, she learned about political and military matters.

When Amina was sixteen years old, her mother, Queen Bakwa Turunku, inherited the throne. She was a powerful ruler, thanks to her father who taught her leadership skills.

The Queen took Amina under her wing, training her in warfare until she became a seasoned warrior.

# CHAPTER FOUR: HEIR APPARENT

When she turned 18, Amina was declared the heir apparent and made part of the ruling cabinet.

Unfortunately, her mother Queen Bakwa died the same year. However, instead of Amina being crowned queen, the men in charge appointed her brother Karama instead. Amina's brother became King Karama.

8

Immediately after he had assumed power, King Karama set out to expand his territory by waging war against states around Zazzau. He took control of new territories, four of which were led by Princess Amina.

Even though King Karama conquered territories under Amina's control, she gained fame as a great warrior. She was fearless in battle. Amina established herself as the only female head of the Zazzau cavalry.

King Karama, died after ruling for ten years.

By then, Princess Amina had proven her worth as a great warrior. The people trusted in her leadership, so they crowned her the next ruler.

The people of Zazzau were very talented at tanning, weaving, and metalwork, often setting out on long journeys to sell their crafts across the Sahara region. They often encountered robbers or slave traders and were frequently killed or captured.  For Queen Amina, the safety of her people was important. She trained the traders, both men and women, to fight. For extra protection, she also sent guards along with them whenever they travelled for trade.

12

Within a very short time, she gathered an army of 20,000 foot soldiers and one thousand cavalry troops and began her first expedition. The highly-trained soldiers were fearless fighters. As they conquered city after city, Zazzau became the most powerful city-state of the region.

Thanks to her conquests, she captured a large tract of land, which helped to spread her domain as far north and south of the region as it could reach. At the same time, she also created new trade routes throughout Northern Africa, connecting western Sudan with Egypt and Mali.

In those days, the people of Zazzau lived in huts without protection, making them susceptible to attacks; the queen ingeniously birthed an idea.

She built 'ganuwar' or walls of mud around Zazzau; she also posted guards on the walls securing the city. She set out to fortify the areas around the newly acquired cities she had conquered, thus marking and protecting them from invaders.

# CHAPTER NINE: QUEEN AMINA'S DOMINION

Queen Amina's 34 years reign were spent fighting wars and expanding her territories. She established her dominance over a large area of land and brought in massive wealth, making her city the center of trade and commerce.

Queen Amina also introduced the use of metal armor like iron helmets and chain mail as protection against enemies. For this reason, she was nicknamed "the iron mail queen."

18

Queen Amina died in 1610 at the age of 77. Parts of her home, "Ganuwar Amina" (Amina's walls), still remain standing, carrying on her legacy even to the present day.

She was the first woman to become queen in a male-dominated society. The Queen Amina Statue was first erected in 1975 at the entrance to the National Arts Theatre in Lagos, Nigeria, in memorial of a legend and a symbol of strength, great warrior and great leader.

20

# REFERENCES


- "Queen Amina-1533-1610" Encyclopedia.com
https://www.encyclopedia.com/history/news-wires-white-papers-and-books/queen-amina

- "Queen Amina of Zaria" Biography.com
https://biography.yourdictionary.com/amina-of-zaria

- Queen Amina of Zazzau: A West African Warrior Queen BlackHistoryHeros.com
http://www.blackhistoryheroes.com/2013/07/queen-amina-of-zaira-west-african.html
https://our-ancestories.com/queen-amina/

# ACKNOWLEDGEMENTS

For her  work on and support of this book, to Marjy Marj, (Marjorie Boafo Appiah).

For guiding the manuscript through the copyediting phase, thanks to Letitia deGraft Okyere.

For his tireless efforts at formatting and design, thanks to Nasim Malik Sarkar.

# ABOUT AUTHOR

Rosemond Sarpong Owens is a diversity, equity & inclusion professional. She has a passion for history and storytelling and is inspired to share stories of heroes and heroines of African descent. Sarpong Owens is a wife and mother to three girls who love to read. She hopes that this book encourages children to be proud of themselves and their heritage.

# PLEASE LEAVE A REVIEW

Please take a moment to rate and review Queen Amina
as this helps others (kids, parents, teachers) discover her
story. I love hearing from my readers.

Thank You!

# OTHER BOOKS IN THE HERITAGE COLLECTION

The story of Yaa Asantewaa is one of courage and the survival of a kingdom and its people. As a brave warrior, she motivated her people to defend themselves in the fight against British colonialism. Today, many parents name their children in her honor.

Who was Queen Nandi? She is referred to as one of the greatest mothers that ever lived. As a queen mother, she saw her son Shaka become one of the greatest kings of the Zulu people and builder of the Zulu empire. Read her story and learn how she made her mark in history.

Eléni was a Princess from Hadiya who became the wife of Emperor Zara Yaqob in 1445. Eléni guided the reign of five emperors and fearlessly challenged the leading role men played in society as an Empress, Queen Mother and Regent. Eléni's story will inspire girls and women everywhere to rise above difficult circumstances and fulfill their destiny.

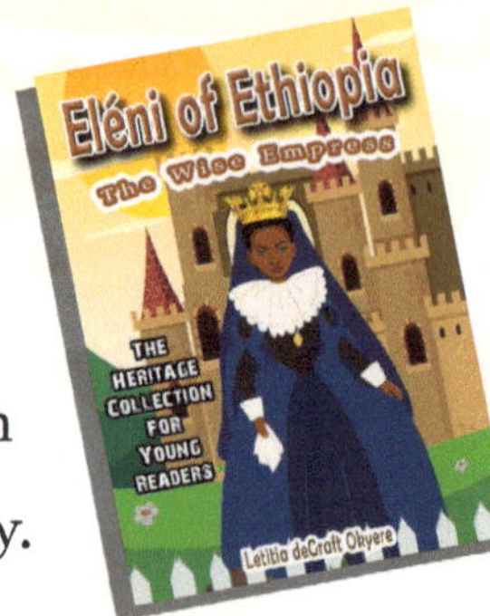

www.ingramcontent.com/pod-product-compliance
Lightning Source LLC
Chambersburg PA
CBHW042203030726
47602CB00007B/106